TOOLS FOR SLOW LIVING

A PRACTICAL GUIDE
TO MINDFULNESS
& COZINESS

TABLE OF CONTENTS

TO RELAX

DECKCHAIR 016
HAMMOCK 020
BIKE 024
SWIMSUIT 028
TICKET 032
BLANKET 036
TRAINERS 040
BACKPACK 044
ARMCHAIR 048
SOFA 052
FLIP-FLOPS 056

TO SOCIALIZE

WICKER BASKET	120
BOULE	124
CHESS	128
TENT	132
PICNIC BASKET	136
ICE BAG®	140
TABLE	144
BARBECUE	148
COOKBOOK	152
PHOTO ALBUM	156

TO ENTERTAIN

BOOK 162
MAPS 166
ANALOGUE CAMERA 170
GRAMOPHONE 174
POTTER'S WHEEL 178
POTS FOR HERBS 182
SEWING MACHINE 186
COLOURING BOOK XXL 190
JIGSAW PUZZLE 194
BALLOON 198

SLOW DOWN

All we want nowadays is to pack as many things into our schedules as possible. It is rare that we are not trying to do several things at once, even though multitasking is not really effective. We dream about squeezing even more into our to-do lists. Taking a moment to rest, evaluate or think is not an option. Driven by the fear of missing out, we want to be everywhere, or at least somewhere, at any time. Always in a hurry, we never have a moment to contemplate or simply to get bored. Many of us lead this kind of life from our early years.

Actually, the more we learn, achieve or work, the more we want. We want the best within the same or an even shorter timeframe. It is like being trapped in a vicious cycle. Technological advances instead of helping our everyday lives, speed everything up and make it even more complicated. While it is truly fabulous to be able to communicate with someone cross the globe in real time, we certainly let our devices rule our lives. We have no idea how to use them wisely, so they took control over our routines. Many cannot function without social media and surfing the Web, the virtual reality is the only 'real' world they know. Wifi became our most valuable tool and we can connect anywhere and everywhere 24/7.

Whenever our computers are out of reach, we are glued to mobile screens. Over dinner many family members prefer to chat on-line or browse the Internet rather than to converse with each other. Many of us set out on trips or visit museums to take photos and post them online without really looking at the actual places or artworks. Being on a mission to tick off the list of attractions, there is no time to lose. In short, we are never really mindfully present.

Highly stressed, we pay little or no attention to details. Without digesting current experiences properly, we are always reaching for the next one, in need of

Fast is busy, controlling, aggressive, hurried, analytical, stressed, superficial, impatient, active, quantity-over-quality. Slow is the opposite: calm, careful, receptive, still, intuitive unhurried, patient, reflective, quality-over-quantity. It is about making real and meaningful connections – with people, culture, work, food, everything.

CARL HONORÉ
'In Praise of Slow'

The secret is balance: instead of doing everything faster, do everything at the right speed.

CARL HONORÉ
'In Praise of Slow'

constant stimulation enhanced by media, from other people running at the same tempo, or our delusions about perceiving the world.

We think that our round-the-clock philosophy will allow us to be at the centre of events, but in reality this fast-paced lifestyle leads to confusion and discontent and, in effect, also to aggression or depression. We are totally lost, even if we think that we were never so well informed and equipped. First of all we have lost touch with ordinary life, with each other and last but not least with ourselves. There is so much going on non-stop that we are not even able to process and enjoy any moment that arrives or anybody that we meet on our (high)way. Instead of being in the here and now, we are already planning what we should do next. The 'need for speed' used to be the name of a racing video game, now our contemporary lifestyle can be called the same.

This is a wake-up call! Do not be a lunatic on the way to burnout. It is still possible to enjoy life at a normal pace again. There are many things in life that cannot be rushed, so take your time. We wish to inspire you to stop racing against the clock and get back the forgotten art of relaxation, be it by yourself, while practicing your hobbies or sharing time and positive energy with others. Gathered here are objects and accessories that will teach you how to relax again, enjoy simple moments, share them with loved ones, some will also inspire new hobbies and entertainments. Sit back, relax and learn from our collection of tools for slow living and escape the hurly-burly of everyday life. You will see that exercising the slow mode will let you re-discover a happy and gratifying life.

TO RELAX

DECKCHAIR

Its name comes from the fact that they were originally used on the decks of cruise ships as a place for travellers to enjoy some sun while on board. (Some were reserved for particular passengers and had name tags on the back.) The ill-fated 'Titanic' offered no less than 600 wooden deckchairs, six of which are known to have survived.

The chair with its simple construction, consisting of a frame, a single strip of fabric (originally canvas) and two foldable legs, is light and easy to move. The classic deckchair can be locked in only one position and when does not take up much storage space. Some designers were re-working its iconic shape, but even with additional elements like a leg- or an armrest, the idea is the same. Folding chairs as such were even known in the Bronze Age and in ancient cultures. The contemporary versions, patented in 1855 in the US by John Cham, were used on ocean liners from the 1860s. Across the Atlantic, in the UK, John Thomas Moore patented a portable folding chair in 1886, which was also used on ships as well as on lawns across Great Britain. (Thought to have been introduced by Atkins in the late 19th century, a colony of deckchairs with brightly coloured striped seats is still a common view in English parks every summer.)

Deckchairs became particularly popular in the 20th century and are still widely used. You can easily rent them when spending holidays at the seaside or enjoying lunch in the park. During the summer it is very likely that a deckchair will be your seat if you go to an open-air concert or cinema across the world.

Whether you have a plot of grass next to your home, a beach, a nice park, or a small balcony, there is nothing more rewarding than a half-hour session of relaxing in a deckchair. Enjoy it all year round by wrapping yourself up in a blanket on chillier days.

HAMMOCK

The quintessence of relaxation, a sling made from a piece of fabric with ropes on either end that are wrapped around two points (the hammock is usually suspended between tree trunks). You can take a nap, gaze at the sky, rest or read while swinging gently to calm your nerves, especially over the summer holidays.

The first hammocks were invented for sleeping by Native Americans living in the central and southern parts of the Americas. Their beds, suspended over the ground (safe enough for a night's sleep), were initially woven out of the hamack tree's bark. Who brought them to Europe? It is believed that it was Christopher Columbus on his voyage back to Spain from islands in today's Bahamas. In the following centuries, hammocks were used as beds on sailing ships (they were space savers!) and produced from canvas. Over time they were widely used in camps, holiday resorts and private gardens. Today they come in numerous styles, colours and materials. There is nothing that speaks more of perfect leisure than being cocooned in a hammock lengthwise for a nap or reading a book while sitting across its width. It is scientifically proven that the hammock's rocking motion makes one fall asleep more quickly as well as providing a deeper sleep.

Although they are common worldwide, the hammock culture is particularly popular in El Salvador. There is a valley called 'The Valley of the Hammocks' in San Salvador City. The Native Americans used to sleep there in hammocks due to frequent earthquakes. Even today, you will see hammocks everywhere, often with a Salvadoran taking a nap in it. Each year in November the country organizes 'The Festival of the Hammock'.

If you love the idea of a hammock, but do not have any suspension points within reach, there are many solutions for having it installed on a balcony or even indoors, including a special frame from which the hammock can be suspended.

BIKE

The secret of a happy city? According to Charles Montgomery who has written a book addressing the problem, while driving increases the stress hormones in our body and forces us to stay inactive, cycling can be beneficial in a number of ways. Cities that reduce traffic in favour of cyclists turn not only into healthier places, but also much happier ones. In Copenhagen, the kingdom of the bike, the percentage of cyclists is over 50% and more people use bikes to get to work or anywhere else than any other means of transportation.

Being a good combination of transportation and recreation, bikes have also become a popular way of visiting cities thanks to a series of bike rental networks. While you can rent a bike, it is highly advisable to own one. In 1965 the production of cars and bikes worldwide was around 20 million of each. In 2003 the proportions were much different with 100 million bikes produced and only 42 million cars. Nowadays there are more than a billion bicycles across the globe, so we are moving in the right direction.

The bike was created in the 19th century as the result of a series of innovations in such experimental vehicles such as the draisienne and velocipede. The frame, at first wooden then iron, plus pedals, rubber tires of equal size, gears and cable-pull brakes were developed along the way to produce the bicycle we use today. Many fanciful designs have been introduced, but classical models are still trendy, too. The bike is the perfect way to move more quickly than walking, have a more natural connection with the surrounding, and to enjoy a refreshing breeze while pedalling.

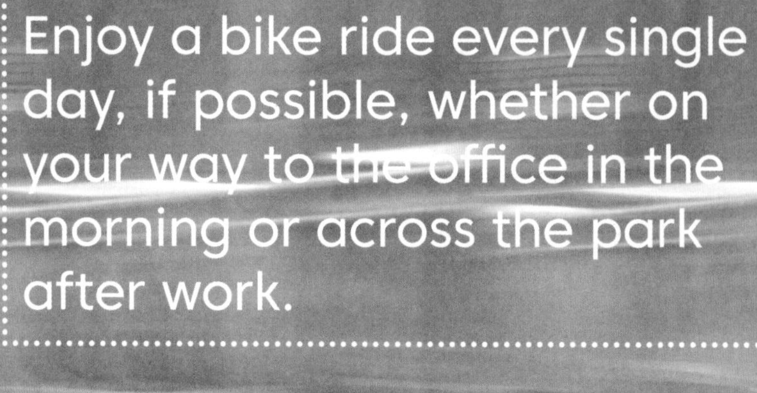

Enjoy a bike ride every single day, if possible, whether on your way to the office in the morning or across the park after work.

SWIMSUIT

The days when you used to be promptly arrested for indecent exposure for wearing a revealing swimsuit are long gone. There are no more beach censors whose job it was to measure if swimsuits followed strict regulations. As morals changed over the decades, so did the form of a swimsuit. The evolution of this accessory went from almost totally covering the body to exposing nearly all of it. In 1825 women not only had to wear so-called bathing dresses on the beach, they also used bathing machines bringing them directly to the water without exposing them to the public eye. One hundred years later Hollywood stars popularized bathing suits, although they were still considered provocative. Today our standards of modesty are less strict and, provocatively, we tend to barely cover our bodies at all.

When the French designer Louis Réard designed the 'Bikini' back in 1946, he was unable to find a fashion model to wear the suit. Eventually a nude casino dancer promoted the new style which soon dominated beaches around the globe. How times have changed is evidenced by the world's largest bikini parade organized in November 2009 in Johannesburg. Its aim was to raise awareness of breast cancer in Africa.

Whatever type of swimsuit you prefer, be it a one-piece or a bikini, it is associated with swimming or sun bathing as well as with the pleasure of summer or holidays. Our bodies trapped in clothes in everyday life (unless you work as a lifeguard), love the moment of changing into a swimsuit with its promise of freedom for the body. Our skin enjoys the exposure to water or sun (or both) allowing the body to drift a slow mode of relaxation.

Pack your bathing suit and, depending on the time of the year, find the closest water reservoir or your local swimming pool. Have a swim.

TICKET

We all know that moment when winter seems to have lasted just a bit too long and we are fed up with the cold temperatures, and many layers of clothes. What we were looking forward to at the end of a hot summer now just irritates us instead of bringing relief. We are constantly tired, drink too much coffee to stay awake and miss the energy and warmth of the sun. This is exactly when travel agencies start bombarding us with special offers, as everyone knows it's high time to plan a holiday.

Buying a ticket is obviously only the first step, but what an important one! Once we decide where and when we wish to escape the burdens of our everyday lives (not necessarily only in winter), the prospect of upcoming trip can seriously brighten our days. A ticket is a chance to break our routine, experience something new and take some time off. A good work-life balance is crucial for a healthy life, but so is charging our batteries while traveling and exploring new places. Be it a one-day trip somewhere nearby or a week-long holiday on a tropical island or a weekend city break, a ticket is a promise of adventure.

Especially now that buying a ticket has never been so easy. E-tickets, particularly for airline travel, are a matter of a few clicks, which has only been possible since the mid-90s (while paper tickets are still available, some airlines charge a fee for issuing them). Whether you travel by plane, train, bus or ferry, each carrier has a website and booking is available 24/7. You can plan your next trip sitting comfortably at home. Grab a ticket and enjoy the pleasures that travelling provides.

Po
G. v.
Genua

Regardless of the time of the year, or how busy you are at this moment, just sit down and pick your next destination. As soon as you make the choice, buy the ticket. No re-booking or changing your mind is allowed!

VS
744
763
JUL
SATURDAY
M80
15JUL
SATURDAY
ITTINERARY NUMBER

BLANKET

You can lead a slow life on one main condition—that you say no to rush. One of the most pleasant ways to do so is by having a siesta during the day. Whether it is a weekend or a working day, be it in summer or winter, a morning or an afternoon nap can create miracles. Even fifteen minutes spent snoozing relaxes the body and refreshes the mind. It is believed to increase creativity, boost productivity and reduce stress.

Many historical figures napped regularly to power through long days. Leonardo da Vinci is said to have taken 15-minutes naps every four hours! Winston Churchill once said: "Nature has not intended mankind to work from eight in the morning until midnight without that refreshment of blessed oblivion which, even if it only lasts 20 minutes, is sufficient to renew all the vital forces." And as we all agree that napping has quite a few health benefits, it is hard to imagine lying down without also wanting a cozy covering in which to wrap ourselves. Blankets come in many types of material and decorative patterns, so can be chosen to fit both your interior and the time of the year.

While in winter we cover up for warmth, innovative technologies have given us blankets that keep the body cool in summer. It is a well-known fact that children adore being wrapped in a cozy blanket. Embraced in a woven cloth, they feel secure. Adults need this comfort just as much as the little ones (no wonder the term 'blanket' is often interchanged with 'comforter'). Another idea is to enjoy lazy evenings under a blanket snuggled up to your loved one. Last but not least, a blanket can be used for a picnic, a reading session or simply for enjoying being outdoors. Spread on the grass it will bring you closer to what's natural and relaxing.

Feeling fatigued? Boost your mood by grabbing your favorite blanket and enjoying a regenerating nap or a cozy evening. Not only today or tonight, make it a regular habit.

TRAINERS SNEAKERS

Even if trainers, also known as sneakers, were initially designed for practicing sports or physical exercise, we wear them in everyday life more than ever. Why? The answer is simple: You will not find a more comfortable pair of shoes on this planet. A great relief to our feet, they provide flexibility and softness, not to mention that they allow us to move quickly.

A look back... The first innovation involved the rubber-soled shoes nicknamed plimsolls (relating to the Plimsoll line on a ship's hull, similarly in a shoe if water gets above the line of the rubber sole, the foot gets wet). The first running shoes were designed in 1895 by the British company J. W. Foster and Sons. In the 1930s, athletic shoes became popular among the general public and were not only worn by sportsmen. Interestingly, various designs were made available for both men and women. Fifty years later sneakers have become a part of rock'n roll and hip hop culture.

Over time the materials and structures of the shoes have evolved to give as much comfort as possible. Our lifestyle has also changed significantly and with more opportunities for leisure as well as less demanding dress codes, more and more people choose trainers as an important part of their outfit. These days we can not only get shoes designed especially for a particular kind of sport like jogging, basketball or hiking, but also choose among the many models made for the urban environment. The sight of a gentleman in a suit wearing matching trainers or an elegant lady choosing sneakers over stylish high-heels is not uncommon anymore. The shoes have become much more than simple footwear. Wearing trainers today is a fashion statement and brands, to our advantage, compete in using the most advanced technologies and innovative designers.

Dive into your wardrobe and find a pair of trainers. Next select a picturesque itinerary for a long, relaxing walk and let your feet lead you.

BACKPACK RUCKSACK

Does the memory of your last backpack date back to school days? If not with the student life, do you associate it with excursions into nature? All wrong! Backpacks are so much more and today they have experienced a renaissance. As well as using them for recreational activities or for classes, backpacks are very useful in everyday urban life. Whether carrying your laptop or getting around on a bike, a backpack always comes in handy. Joking apart, it not only offers maximum mobility, but there is also no healthier way to carry things for your spine. Sitting practically on your shoulders, a backpack can contain all you need keeping your hands free (not to mention that it is much better to have the weight distributed across your back than carried in your hands, especially for long distances and periods of time). Numerous brands have re-designed this very traditional object, so it is available in many styles and sizes to match any lifestyle.

Whether you are a sportive type, consider yourself a hipster, wear a suit to work or are a fan of high-heels, you can find a backpack that will be in harmony with your style. What used to be a cloth sack now takes original and sophisticated forms. And thanks to a range of materials, including the most innovative ones, it can be both useful and beautiful. Already known in ancient times, it was used by hunters to carry their prey. Today we use the backpack as an accessory that completes our look. Concerning the word's origination: while backpack comes from American English (the term was said to be coined in the 1910s), the word rucksack is borrowed from German (*Rücken* means 'back' and *Sack* a 'bag').

There are hundreds of backpacks on the market at the moment, from super practical to fashion-oriented ones. Research online or visit a couple of shops and you will be sure to find one to match your style.

ARMCHAIR

Imagine the moment you come back home after a long day at work. You take a shower, put on some casual clothes, turn on the music you like and then recline in a super comfortable armchair, be it with your favourite magazine or a cup of coffee. A pleasant recovery guaranteed! As armchairs are popular elements of furniture, this relaxing scenario can also be carried out in a lesser form when visiting friends, going to cafés or even in waiting rooms. You can always benefit from the inviting shape of an armchair that has been invented to provide exceptional comfort.

A chair is probably the most common piece of furniture. Known from antiquity, it has been used in practically any kind of space – in the kitchen, working areas, children's room, public space or garden to name but a few. To make the seating experience more comfortable, special padding as well as armrests were added. These innovations in the structure made a huge difference and began an era of furniture being so much more than just a useful object. Interestingly, it was an armchair that also gave rise to the sofa.

Designers compete to deliver more and more original models to meet the demands of our stylish contemporary interiors and busy lifestyles. They also experiment with innovative materials and the newest technologies to provide a piece of furniture that will be as practical as it is pleasurable for the body. As it does not require a lot of space, one can accommodate it in even a small room. Sometimes finding the perfect armchair for our needs may take time (despite the number of available designs), but the effort is definitely worth making.

Sit back in your armchair. Forget about the stress of the day, your current worries or obligations. It is just you and your body relaxing in the embracing shape of the backrest. Grab something to read or something to sip, or both and relax. You don't have an armchair at home? Follow the same instructions in your favourite café.

SOFA

If you are in the mood for relaxation in even greater comfort or you have company, a simple armchair will not suffice. You need a proper sofa. The sofa actually originated as curious combinations of armchairs. While a type of sofa was evident in ancient Egypt back in 2000 BC, after the fall of the Roman Empire this comfortable piece of furniture was forgotten for over one thousand years. In the late 17th century, European craftsmen tired of using benches or stools as seating, began to develop sofas as we know them today. Initially very expensive due to upholstery and padding, in the 19th century sofas became much more affordable.

The design process has evolved rapidly over the centuries, enhanced by technological advances. Sofas were becoming more and more comfortable and aesthetically diverse. Today manufacturers pay special attention to this exceptionally pleasing piece of furniture. Contemporary designers are commissioned by them to keep up with our modern lifestyles and offer a tremendous choice of designs. Many are as flexible as they are comfortable so we can enjoy a super sofa even if we do not have much space (many of them can also act as beds to maximize their usefulness even more).

A sofa seems to be a must in household furnishing. Can you imagine a living space without one? A place for reading, relaxation, watching movies, taking a nap or as a playground for the young ones. We use sofas in so many ways! Settling down into one, whether on one's own or with friends and family, is a nesting experience. Embraced by a cozy backrest or stretched out on a large seating area, we can feel at our ease as we settle down. There is no better piece of furniture for unwinding.

Wherever you are reading this book, if it is not your sofa, move there. Enjoy the slow mode by immersing yourself into its cushions.

FLIP-FLOPS

The newest studies show that wearing flip-flops may damage your feet. The claim is that walking long distances in flip-flops can injure your Achilles tendon or even alter your natural stride resulting in shin splints and lower back pain. But so long as you use them short-term and do not wear them to run or hike), you can enjoy this symbol of summer style. (It is also advised to get a pair that is slightly bigger than the size of your foot. They are easy to slip on and allow your feet to breathe properly. You obviously cannot walk fast in flip-flops so slowing down your usual pace is inevitable, which makes them a perfect tool for slow living!

Simpler sandals could not exist: a flat sole together with a Y-shaped strap to hold the foot, which characteristically fits between the first and second toes. Flip-flops were known and worn in ancient Egypt (they are featured in some mural paintings from 4000 BC!), but their modern incarnation is based on the Japanese *zōri* brought to the United States by soldiers returning from World War II. In the 1950s and 1960s this casual footwear became very popular, particularly on the west coast, and eventually became an essential part of the beach scene.

The playful name used in American and British English relates to the sound the shoes make when walking in them, however they are called by different names in other countries. Flip-flops can be made from a variety of materials and despite a very simple design, they come in many colours and with various decorations. The most famous design has been produced since 1962 by the Brazilian brand Alpargatas, and is widely known as Havaianas. Flip-flops are THE summer shoes. You can wear them with shorts, a bathing suit or a summer dress.

Whenever the weather allows, wear your flip-flops at least several times per week. After work and over the weekend they will always provide a foretaste of holidays. In winter, you can wear them at home.

TO ENJOY A MOMENT

BATHTUB

People divide into those who prefer a shower and those who would never give up the bath. A long and shallow tub filled with pleasantly warm water, in which you can lie and wind down. Its relaxing qualities were clear to the people living in 3000 BC in the Indus River Valley. Ancient plumbing systems included bathtubs, some of which were personalized in terms of size. (The oldest surviving one was made of hard pottery and discovered at the Knossos Palace complex on Crete, and had quite an exceptional water-management system).

While the ritual of bathing was also known in the Roman Empire, after its collapse it wasn't until the early 19th century that a sewerage system was re-introduced in Europe, so people had to wait for a proper bath tub. When tubs re-emerged, they were first filled with hot water carried back and forth in buckets, then later directly from a tap and emptied through a system of pipes. For a long time, it was a fashionable pleasure only the aristocracy could afford.

The development of sewerage systems at the turn of the 19th and 20th centuries and the fact that it was becoming less expensive to install them, allowed more people to have a bath tub at home. Be it made from steel, cast iron, enamel, wood or plastic; be it a free-standing model with claw feet or a built-in with an apron on the front; rectangular, oval or triangular, bath tubs come in many styles. While a 'whirlpool tub' or 'jacuzzi' with air bubbles has been extremely popular since the late 1960s, Eastern cultures know yet another variation. It is called 'ofuro' in Japanese, you can only bathe while sitting up and thus these bathtubs are short and deep.

Make yourself a bubble bath! Select a soothing fragrance, pour in warm water at your preferred temperature and immerse yourself in the foam. You can light candles to create an ambiance and take a book or a glass of wine with you. Relaxation granted!

BALCONY

It is an escape for some of flat owners and the only substitute for an outdoor experience, particularly welcome during the warm months. Even if you own a garden, having a balcony, or its bigger version such as a terrace, makes life more pleasant as it also gives you a bonus in the form of a view and some privacy. A balcony, especially when furnished with comfortable pieces of furniture and decorated with colourful plants, can easily be transformed into a perfect hideaway.

Styling your balcony means selecting proper and, more importantly, super-comfortable pieces of furniture. A wide range of deckchairs, lounge chairs, tables, cushions or carpets can turn the balcony into a small heaven. Arrange them so that you maximise your comfort. As this is a place to spend many relaxing moments, no matter what size the balcony is, make sure you build a lovely nest. If it has an open plan and there is no roof, you can hide from the sun under a decorative umbrella or an adjustable sunblind, which you can fold away on windy days. There are many designs that will optimize the effect while using the available space. Last but not least, think of plants. Contact with nature, even on a small scale, can be extremely beneficial. While plants and flowers (and in some cases also small trees) provide aesthetic pleasure, you can also consider planting a small herb garden. Depending on the available space, fresh basil, rosemary or parsley can enhance your cooking.

Probably the most famous balcony is located in Verona. Even if Shakespeare mentioned only a window in his 'Romeo and Juliet', romantics keenly attributed a picturesque balcony in an antique villa to the romantic scene. Yet another practical use for a balcony!

Arrange your balcony so that you can sit or eat on it (if it is tiny, foldable chairs or tables are always a good option).

SWING

The *Gangneung Danoje* Festival, designated by UNESCO as a 'Masterpiece of the Oral and Intangible Heritage of Humanity', is a very special tradition in Korea. Scheduled on the 5th of May in the lunar calendar, its celebration includes the swinging contest on a geune (a traditional Korean swing). It is one of the most popular folk games women enjoy during the festival. They build up momentum as they sway back and forth on a swing hung from a tree and the winner is the one who makes the swing go highest. This example shows that the joy of swinging is not reserved exclusively for the young.

You do not need a lot, just a piece of wood, plastic or fabrics (a tire can work, too) and two ropes to fix it to a sturdy branch. Even better if you can find charming scenery and a particularly nice tree to suspend the swing from, then you can relish the pure pleasure of 'flying' through the air, just as we did in childhood. Set in the swing in motion using our legs (bent towards the back when the swing moves forward, straighten towards the front on the backward movement) it works in the same way as a pendulum.

A swing is a special tool for slow living. It makes us feel a liberating lightness and freedom. Gentle puffs of wind brushing our cheeks are part of the fun of swinging higher and higher, up to the limit. Swinging allows you to cherish the moment, offering an unusual physical exercise that also takes us back in time. We can feel again like our small selves, when all that matters was who makes it higher, breaks the record and defies gravity. The joy of swinging lets you forget all your worries, only the sky is the limit.

Find a nice tree with branches high above the ground, install a swing and off you go!

SUNGLASSES

The history of sunglasses is quite interesting. First, there are some mentions of the Roman Emperor Nero wearing polished green emerald gemstones over his eyes while watching the Gladiators. Next, in the 12th century the Chinese invented primitively shaped frames, which held slabs of smoked quartz. They not only blocked the blinding rays of light, but also were keenly used by Chinese judges to stay emotionally detached (Italian courtrooms took this habit over in the 15th century).

In the 18th century, English optician James Ayscough experimented with tinted blue and green lenses, innovations which laid the foundation for modern sunglasses. In the 1930s the optical company Bausch & Lomb invented a special dark-green tint for eyeglasses for the Army to protect pilots. In 1936 Edwin H. Land, who established the Polaroid Corporation, introduced glasses that protected against UV rays, proving that sunglasses were as advisable for health as they were fashionable. One year later Bausch & Lomb created a new and soon-to-be iconic brand Ray-Ban (from banning the sun-rays). Also designed at that time were 'aviators', using the innovative polarized lens technology, worn by American pilots and militaries as well as Hollywood actors and remain the most iconic model even today.

And so sunglasses have become a trendy fashion accessory, and are an important element of style, not only during the summer. Initially worn for the beach, they are now indispensable whenever we leave the house. Why do sunglasses present themselves as one of the tools for slow living? Well, you can enjoy being in the sun, profit from the rays interacting with your skin and producing vitamin D and form a nice brown tan (always using sun cream, of course), but without the frustration caused by squinting in the bright light. Imagine driving, skiing, walking or biking without sunglasses on your nose... it's no-go.

On sunny days never leave the house without your sun-glasses in your pocket.

If the sun hides behind a cloud, wear them nonchalantly on the top of your head.

STRAW HAT

What do Vincent van Gogh, Harold Lloyd, Queen Elizabeth, and Madonna have in common, other than long-lasting popularity? They have all worn remarkable straw hats. These hats, however, do not necessarily make you an instant celebrity. For centuries, they were, in fact, the summer attribute of European peasants working in the fields, as immortalised in Bruegel's painting "The Harvesters".

Their light structure allowed the air to circulate while the hat itself provided protection from the burning sun, but not from rain. Only in the middle of the 19th century, thanks to the popularity of seaside resorts, did the straw hat emerge as fashionable headwear for the higher social classes, as you can see, for example, in some of Renoir's paintings. It diversified in shape, with the launch of the Panama hat in the late 1850s, followed by the boater at the turn of the century, and many more. Not only the shapes, but also the colours and decorative elements added to the diversity. In the USA, Straw Hat Day (officially in mid-June), when men switched from their winter felt hats to their straw equivalents, was seen as the beginning of the summer season. It was widely celebrated throughout the first half of the 20th century.

Nowadays, straw hats are a must-have when you go to the beach or for biking. Take any gossip magazine in the summer, and you will see celebrities hiding, or trying to hide under eccentric straw hats. They are still made of natural straw, although synthetic materials would be softer on the skin, but they do not offer the pleasant smell of fresh straw, and do not absorb humidity as straw does. Keep the plastic straw for your favourite cocktail and enjoy the summer in the shade of your natural, fancy hat.

Simply get one.

BINOCULARS

The pace of life today is rapid. Being constantly in a hurry to get from one point to another, we do not have time to stop and look around. We just speed ahead without really getting to know our surroundings. Binoculars, used to observe remote objects and scenes, have been known since the 17th century when the invention of the telescope revolutionized terrestrial exploration as well as astronomy. Initially binoculars belonged to the equipment of geographers and scientists, but over time the tool became common among nature lovers as a perfect way to watch birds and among amateur astronomers to view the stars.

Today's binoculars are available in more advanced versions depending on how they will be used. How far we can see depends on the field of view, which is determined by its optical design. While they magnify the view with their lenses, you can usually set the focus on a particular element in the distance. Some binoculars have a special image-stabilization feature, which is a good solution for long lasting observations (try it once and you will see that it is hard to keep your hands still). Lenses can also vary in magnification to cover longer distances.

A pair of binoculars provides a perfect reason to calm down and remain quietly in one place with a proper view. Be it in nature or in an urban space, you can have a lot of fun in spotting interesting details that you would normally never notice. Bird watching, for example, can be engaging as well as fascinating. With binoculars in your hands you will forget about the passage of time and the world around. Watching at the avian acrobatics in the sky can be truly absorbing. Binoculars are definitely a great way to fully appreciate your surroundings, especially when it's nature.

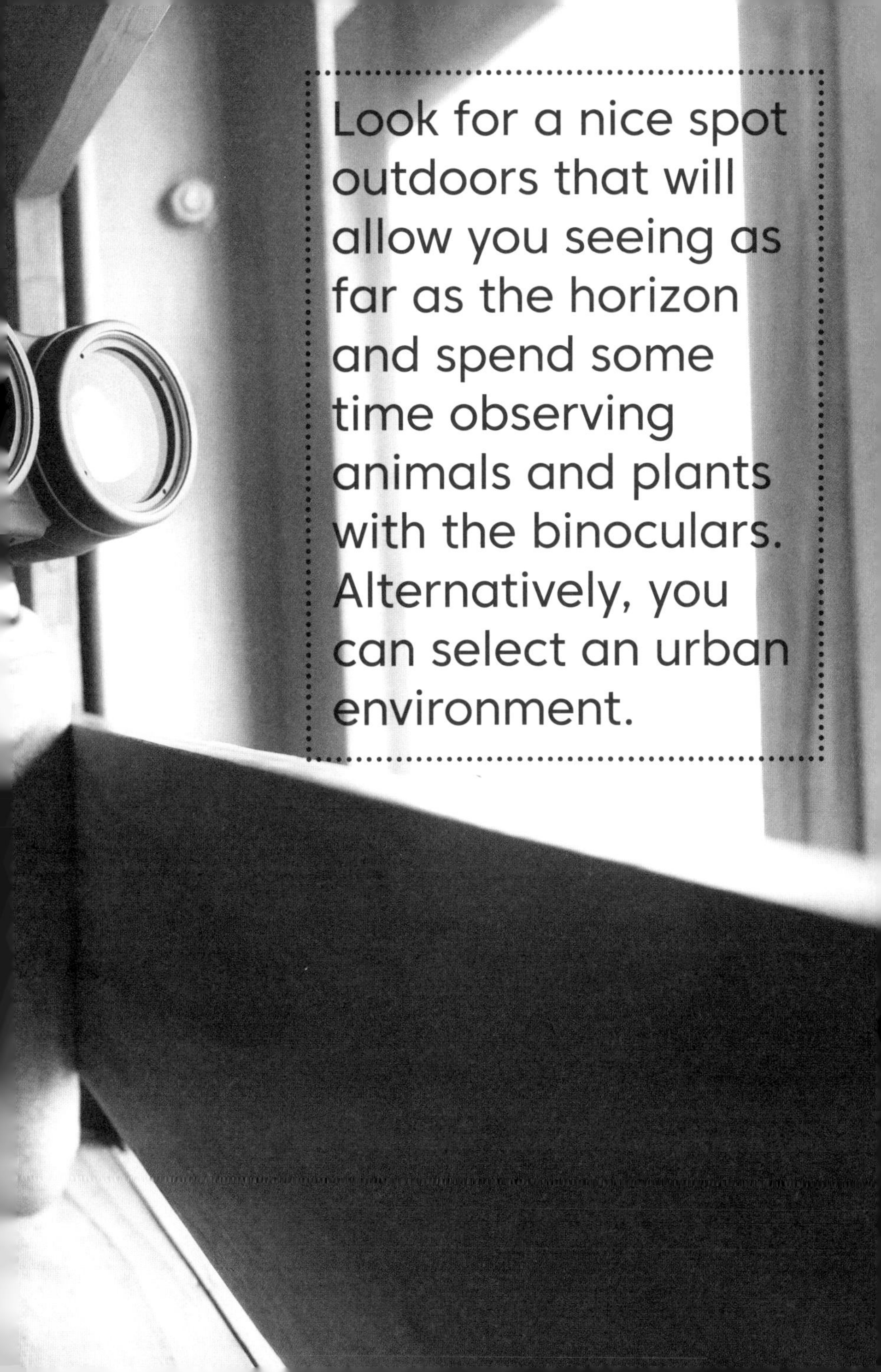

Look for a nice spot outdoors that will allow you seeing as far as the horizon and spend some time observing animals and plants with the binoculars. Alternatively, you can select an urban environment.

A CUP OF COFFEE

Coffee in a glazed ceramic cup so it doesn't cool down too quickly, is synonymous with a moment of gratification. Sipped in company or solitude, it is associated with a break from work, a social meeting or a guilty pleasure. All in all, we love drinking coffee while leafing through a magazine, reading a book or surfing across the Internet. For some reaching for a cup of coffee is the first thing they do in the morning, others are glued to it while working long hours. The best excuse for having another cup is the weather. What could be better on a cloudy and chilly day than a warm and flavourful liquid? That is precisely why a cup of coffee should be a part of your slow collection. Selecting the perfect cup for your coffee is not an easy task. Depending on the quality of the ceramic, its thickness and its size, coffee can taste very different.

Coffeehouses were first introduced by the Ottoman Turks in the middle of the 15th century in Constantinople. When the first one opened in 1475, Turkish law allowed a woman to divorce her husband if he failed to provide her with her daily quota of coffee. Around 1600 coffee was introduced to the West through traders from Italy. New Yorkers started drinking coffee for breakfast instead of beer around 1668, while Paris celebrated its first café in 1672. In 2014 astronauts at the International Space Station used the very first espresso machine in space to have a coffee. Small step for mankind, one giant leap for a man. Given the fact that over 400 billion cups are consumed each year worldwide, the 'coffee culture' could as well be a nickname for our contemporary lifestyle.

Go to your favourite café and enjoy a cup of coffee. Be it cappuccino or espresso, alone or with a friend, make it as you like best.

KAYAK

Kayaks are associated with outdoor life and intrepid explorers, however nowadays it is common to see them in rivers and lakes. Their light structure and manoeuvrability allow them to reach places that ships, or even rafts cannot. Once used by migrating Inuit hunters to follow seals, whose skins were used to cover the whalebone structure, kayaks were promptly adopted by the first Europeans exploring North America, and from there became the perfect tool for enjoying outdoor life on the five continents.

You navigate by using paddles and the current (if there is one), and the kayak seems to glide on the surface of water. Kayaks have one or two cockpits, and, just like skis, longer kayaks are usually faster than the shorter ones. Expect to capsize a couple of times at the beginning – it is part of the fun! A quiet kayak session along the shores of a lake would enable you to observe nature from an unusual viewpoint: it is a perfect place to hear birds, and nature more generally, to spot all shades of green in the landscape, to look at the sky, and to enjoy the calming effect of water. Even the regular paddling contributes to relaxation.

Slow relaxation in a kayak may have various faces. First, depending on whether it's a river or a lake the experience of paddling is different – circling around versus getting from one place to another. On a river, you can start at one point and continue for several days stopping to camp under a tent along the way. Secondly, you can enjoy a kayak on your own but even more with a bunch of your nearest and dearest. It's cool to be together on the water, in the outdoors and get some physical exercise.

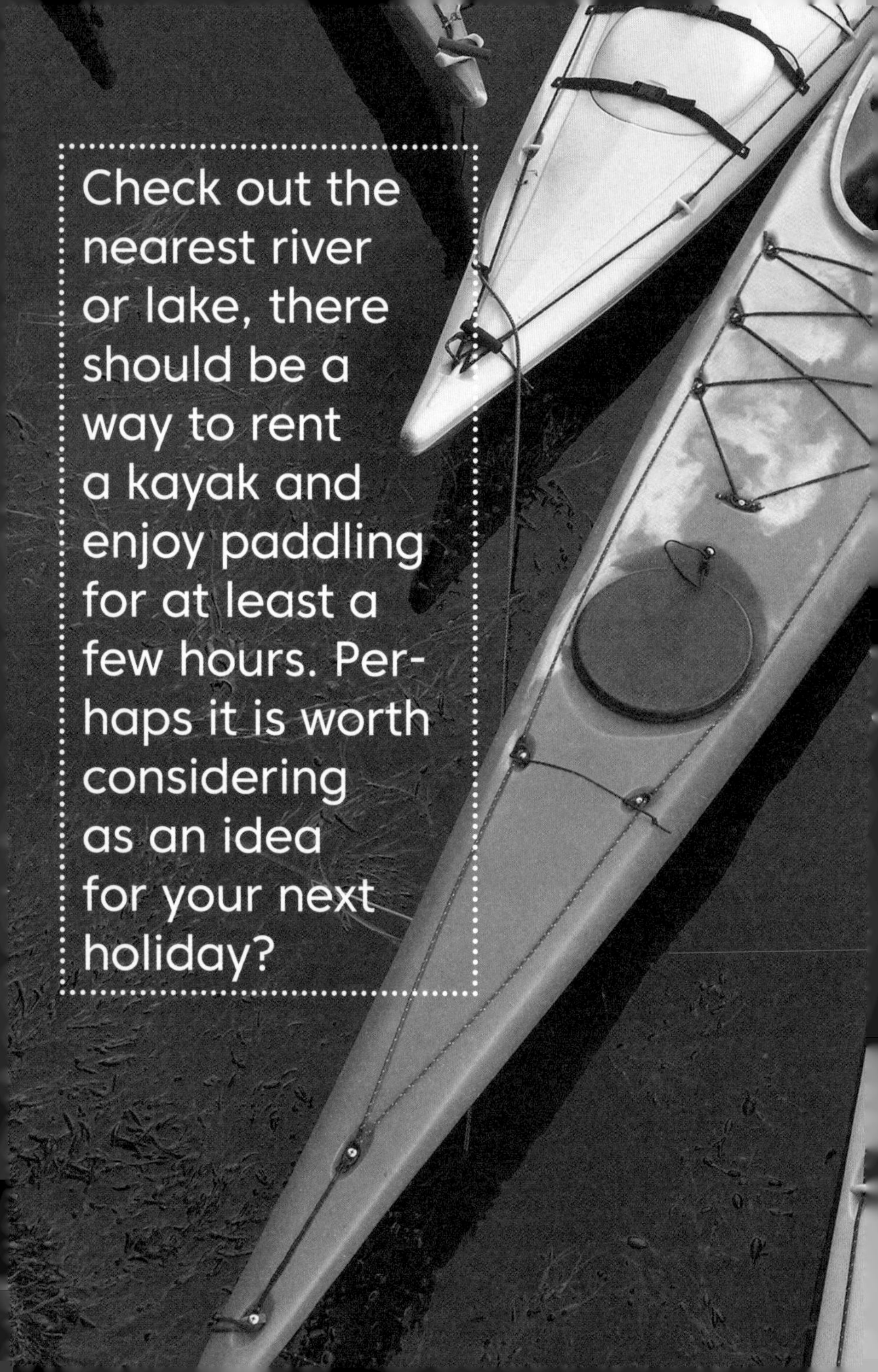
Check out the nearest river or lake, there should be a way to rent a kayak and enjoy paddling for at least a few hours. Perhaps it is worth considering as an idea for your next holiday?

NOTEBOOK

They say that the eyes are windows to the soul, but one could actually say the same about a notebook! Think about all those pages marked with your handwriting, scribbles, doodles or sketches, all of which reflect your personality or mood. Today when we say a notebook, we think of a laptop computer (try to Google the word). But at the same time, despite all the technological advances, we're experiencing an interesting renaissance of notebooks. Paper is certainly not dead! Notebooks come in more and more sizes and shapes, you can select among numerous covers, thicknesses and layouts of the pages. It is not the same to note things on ruled, blank, dotted or squared ones.

Why do we need to make notes at all? Obviously to remember dates, anniversaries, to-do lists, important thoughts, ideas, contact details, etc. Today the most common practice is to use our computers or mobile phones (best if both are well-synchronized) to gather all the data. We can set reminders and alarms, so we never miss anything. BUT imagine your computer's memory suddenly crashes and your mobile somehow lands in your drink. Traditional notebooks will never let you down and they have a soul.

Typing on the touchscreen of one's mobile is quick and computers have an option which guesses and finishes words automatically for you making it faster to type. A notebook is certainly much more demanding. While it takes more time to make a note by hand, you also have a longer moment to think about what you're about to write. Plus it is so nice to feel a pen or a pencil in your hand and take the time to write something down. A notebook also has other advantages. The lack of a 'set an alarm' option, for instance, is a good exercise for your memory.

Get yourself a nice note-
book, a pocket-sized one
you can take everywhere
or a book-format that will
be perfect for bigger ideas,
longer texts or drawings.
Enjoy the traditional art
of taking notes!

FOUNTAIN PEN

Fountain pens are the ultimate vintage chic, a lovely survivor of a lost time, like straight razors, Bakelite objects, or tweed jackets. It is hard to imagine that in the 19th century the same tool was celebrated as a masterpiece of engineering and human inventiveness. It took no less a genius than Leonardo da Vinci to sketch and create a prototype, but as usual with Leonardo da Vinci's ideas, it was way ahead of its time: quills were an inexpensive material and the literacy rate low.

The prototypes of modern fountain pens were developed three centuries later, in the wake of the first industrial revolution. A luxury object throughout the 19th century, the fountain pen contributed to the fame and wealth of companies like Waterman, Parker, and Montblanc. Although fountain pens lost their predominance to ballpoint pens in the 1950s, they never disappeared from the market. Their timeless elegance, the pleasure of tracing letters with them, and the nostalgic touch they confer to writings, make them objects of desire for calligraphy fans, romantic souls and collectors. The fountain pen is a perfect gift for a budding writer or poet. One might have thought that the development of tablets and smartphones would have dealt the *coup de grâce* to the fountain pen, as fewer and fewer people write by hand.

Paradoxically, fountain pens are regaining their popularity – probably because the slow tempo of writing with them allows time to weigh each word before formulating sentences in contrast to the ever-faster way of sending messages without really thinking twice about the phrasing. By using a fountain pen, you not only show more of your personality – as handwriting can reveal your nature – but you also accept slowing down and favouring substance over immediacy.

Instead of sending a text message, use a fountain pen and pay attention to the act of writing. Whenever you have to send a note or sign anything, take your time and enjoy the sensual pleasure of ink on paper.

TEA CUP

Tea, initially used as a curative liquid (or part of religious rituals, such as the powdered green tea used by Buddhist monks), soon became a treat and was drunk for pleasure. This sophisticated and healthy drink, available in many varieties can regenerate, refresh and boost both your body and mind. Although various nations may have different attitudes towards tea, it has become as popular as coffee. Actually tea is the most consumed beverage in the world second only to water. One drinks only the highest quality tea and pays special attention to the traditional ways of preparing it. The Japanese tea ceremony, still performed today, is an excellent example of how the tea culture has survived over the centuries.

Good tea should be prepared in a proper cup as its thickness and material may influence the taste. Each type of tea requires a different treatment or brewing technique: some should be drunk at a particular time of a day, some will become less caffeinated depending on the length of timesteeping and the temperature of the water, some will produce moresubtle flavours.

The custom of drinking tea is worth cultivating in everyday life. You do not necessarily have to follow the complex Japanese tea ceremony, but it is good to make a cup of tea (or a couple) a daily habit. Select the sort(s) of tea you like most and learn how to brew them properly to obtain the optimum flavor and enjoy their healthful qualities. Whether you relish black, green or white teas, become a connoisseur (there are over 3,000 varieties to choose from). Have your favourite cup ready to enjoy your daily quota of tea.

Taste various types of tea, select the ones you like best and take pleasure in drinking them every day. Make sure you drink them at the right times of day and prepare them according to the rules.

CANDLE

Slow living should bring not only comfort and quiet, but also create a special atmosphere for the soul. We cannot imagine a better way to provide it than to light a candle. This simple and centuries-old object is nothing more than an ignitable wick surrounded by wax. In the past candles were used as a source of light (today only sudden electricity cuts remind us of that need) and interestingly, before the invention of electricity candles were more common in Northern Europe while the South and the Mediterranean opted for oil lamps.

A candle is also an inspiring element of interior decoration. Not only can you get candles of all sizes, shapes and colours, but you can also find the most imaginative candle holders for displaying them. Widely popular, especially in countries with long winter evenings, they can also turn summer nights into a special experience. Whether you hide at home from the cold temperatures or celebrate summer outdoors, candles will be great companions, providing a romantic ambiance. A candle-lit dinner, a bath surrounded by candles or a party with lots of candles illuminating the guests are some of the many ways to add some magic to everyday life. And last but not least, for those who like pleasing several senses at once, there are also candles with fragrances.

Time goes by slowly as the candle melts and becomes shorter. It provides light and warmth as well as creating a special ambience of coziness and relaxation. A room or a garden lit by the glow of many candles can look spectacular. While they might not be ideal for reading, illumination by candlelight is somehow romantic, mysterious and atmospheric. The moment you light some candles, you simply switch off and enter the dimension of Zen.

If you decide to experience sensual relaxation on your own, you can place many lit candles around your bathroom and take an aromatic bath. Another idea is to organize a candle-lit dinner where food will be tasted without rushing and in a magical atmosphere. Whether outdoors on a summer night or cozily at home over the winter, it is a gratifying experience.

WELLIES

On a rainy day, it is tempting to stay at home and enjoy lazy hours on the couch. But you would miss the beauty of nature in the rain, particularly in the spring and at the end of the summer, when the smell of humid earth is particularly enjoyable, when you can collect wild flowers, berries, or mushrooms, or observe animals because they expect most humans would avoid the rain.

Rain is when nature comes alive, and a few refreshing drops should not deter you from walking and communicating with nature. Just put on your good old wellies, even if they are still muddy from your last walk in adverse weather conditions, and you will forget about humidity and cold. Rubber boots are an incongruity in terms of fashion and elegance, even if you have the most unobtrusive colour (dark green). So you have a good reason to select a pair with conspicuous patterns and colours.

Wellies owe their name to the first Duke of Wellington, who famously defeated Napoleon at Waterloo wearing a prototype of the waterproof boots that were promptly adopted by the aristocracy for hunting and horse riding sessions. Initially made of calf leather, the wellies were a luxury good until the 1850s, when British-American industrialist, Hiram Hutchison, produced the first rubber wellies, thus making them affordable for a wider clientele. They are easy to put on and to remove, and do not require any polishing at all. Wellies are indeed the best protection against rain, snow, and mud, so you have no excuse to skip a stroll, just put on some warm, rain-proof clothes and your wellies. It is fun to walk in the rain, and you will enjoy a warm drink even more when you get back home.

Take a walk in the rain or shortly after. Your wellies will keep your feet dry and you will be able to benefit from the freshness of the air.

HAND FAN

Does the idea of using a hand-held fan to create a gentle,cooling airflow to cool remind you of historical paintings or sensational flamenco dancers? Perhaps it does, but since it is so practical and refreshing when it is too hot to breathe, why not use it today? Hand fans were known in ancient Greece, but then were long forgotten. It was not until the 16th century when they were re-introduced from Japan. The Japanese fans quickly became very popular, especially among aristocracy. As these fans were often lavishly decorated, ladies liked to be featured in portraits displaying spread fans in their hands. In the 19th century they became an integral part of women's dress. Interestingly while fans are part of dance culture (there is Buchaechum, a Korean fan dance, or Cariñosa, the national dance of the Philippines to name but a few), in Japanese war tradition they were used as weapons.

In the following centuries fans were imported not only from Japan, but also from China or East Indies. But at the same time more and more European craftsmen decided to specialise in manufacturing them. Made of paper, sandalwood or silk, their surface was usually painted, sculpted or decorated with feathers. Over time the artistry of making fans was taken to another level.

Today many modern designs and materials have been introduced and we can re-discover fans anew. In the past, they were very useful in sending secret messages (a special fan language full of coded signs could communicate without breaking strict social etiquette), now a hand fan can also be used in a very practical way. In the age of global warming and as summer days become hotter and hotter, it is important to keep cool. A hand fan is a perfect and sophisticated portable air-con.

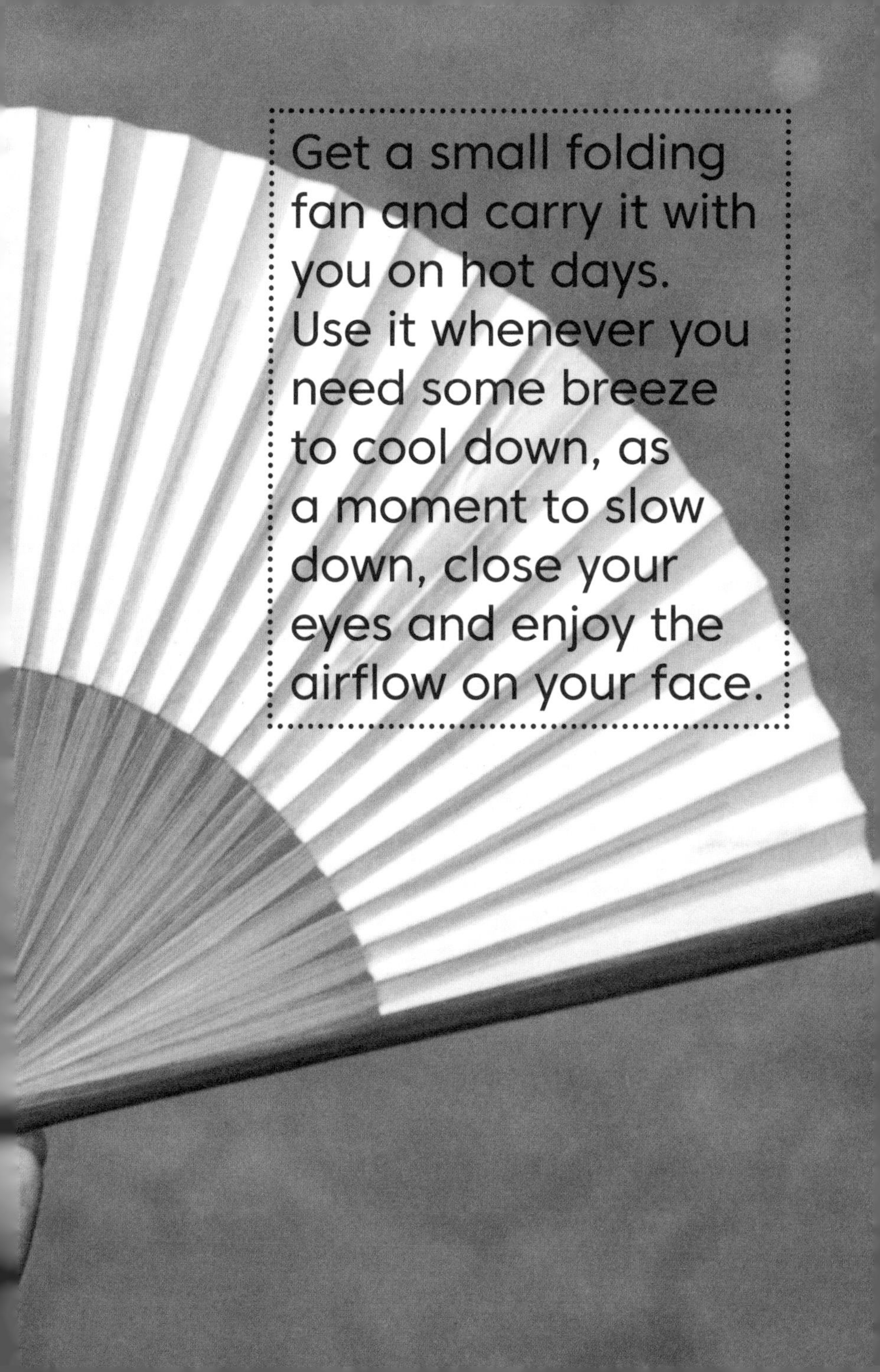

Get a small folding fan and carry it with you on hot days. Use it whenever you need some breeze to cool down, as a moment to slow down, close your eyes and enjoy the airflow on your face.

TO SOCIA

WICKER BASKET

Used to food shopping in soulless supermarkets, we pack the metallic and creaking baskets with products with 'best before' dates. Even if equipped with a shopping list, we are always tempted to buy much more than we intend to, and end up with products we actually do not need. Food is either processed or stuffed with preservatives. If there are any smells, it is the air sprayed with the artificial scent of freshly baked bread scent to make customers feel hungry and thus purchase even more.

Now imagine this. It's France on a lazy and sunny morning. Located in the market square or simply along some streets, is the French *marché* filled with colourful stalls with regional specialties, talkative vendors and most importantly smiling and happy clients. Selecting products, tasting some of them, speaking with the sellers is part of the French *l'art de vivre*. There is no rush, just taking time to please the senses. No canned or vacuum-packed food, only 100 % natural and fresh products (usually straight from the local producer). Buying food like this is so much more inspiring. No shopping list is necessary, all you need is to open your eyes and immerse yourself in the market's atmosphere.

The charm of a traditional French market is an unforgettable experience, once you try it, you will want to come back every day. There are only two conditions. First, you have to take your time and secondly, you need a proper wicker shopping basket. Natural wicker combines aesthetic qualities with those of comfort. This delicate material woven with special techniques is super strong, long-lasting, and lightweight, yet sturdy and flexible. Wicker has been known since Ancient Egyptian times and its handmade tradition still survives. Are you ready to celebrate slow food shopping?

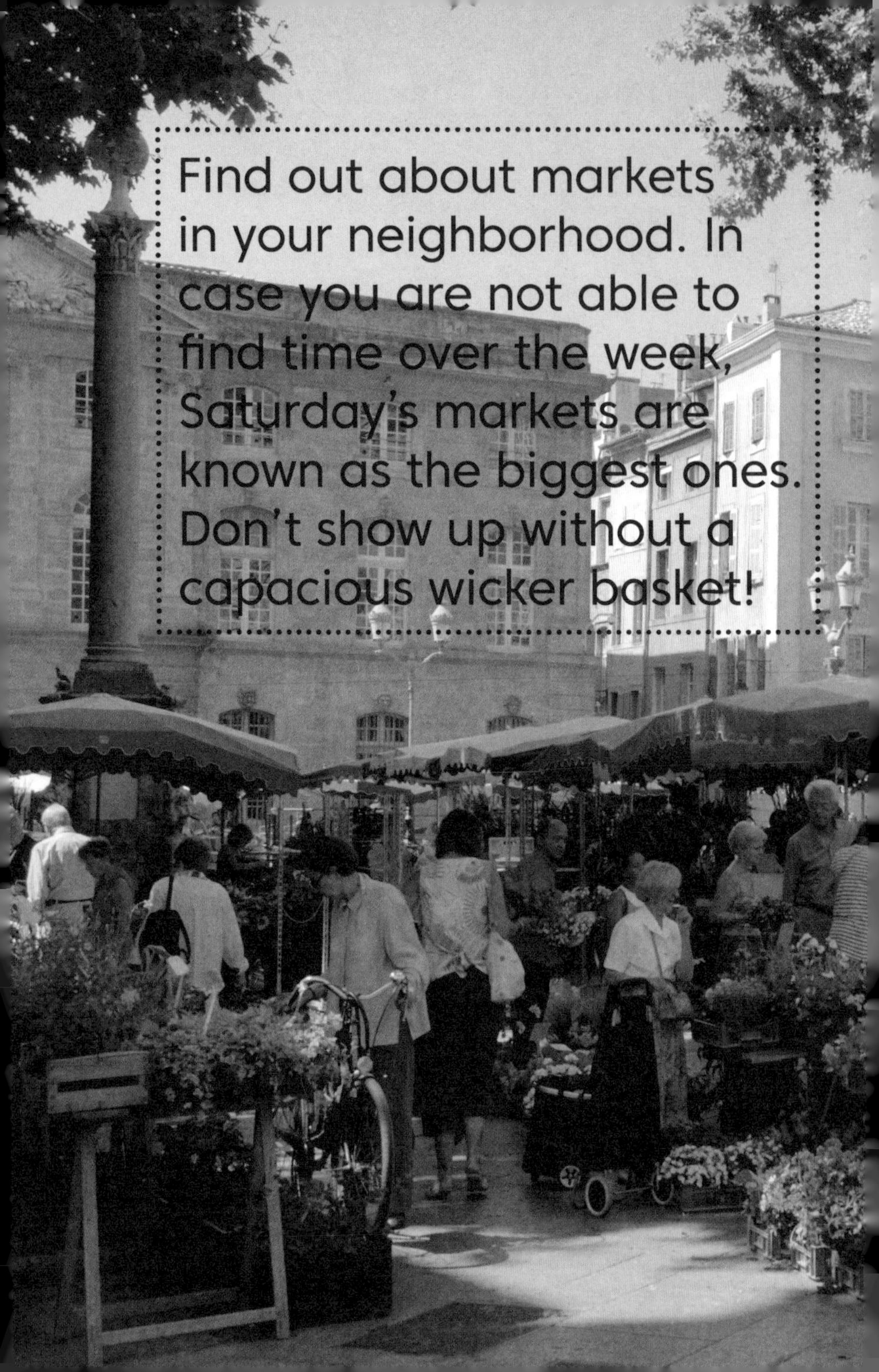
Find out about markets in your neighborhood. In case you are not able to find time over the week, Saturday's markets are known as the biggest ones. Don't show up without a capacious wicker basket!

BOULE

You must have seen a group of people in a park or at a square standing together, talking, laughing and making some unhurried movements from time to time. They lean and throw a ball, some make a short run up before throwing (like in boule Lyonnaise). There is no rush, on the contrary, the players take their time as they want to be precise. This relaxed competition is called 'boule' (a French word for 'ball') and is a perfect team game to soothe the nerves in good company and in open air. The balls one throws in boule are relatively heavy. The idea is to place them as close as possible to a small target that is set at the start. The game is particularly popular across France, but it is also common in Italy. In many cities and villages there are special boule courts with flattened surfaces.

It is believed the game was known in ancient cultures when the balls were made of stone. The Romans spread the game among Gallic tribes and in centuries to come, it became an iconic entertainment in France. In the 19th century the balls were manufactured of hard boxwood root enforced by iron nails. To make them even more durable, they were finally produced entirely of metal. Today you can find sets made of both wood and metal, as well as soft versions for playing indoors. The structure of the ball can also vary.

Boule seems easy, but in fact, you have to evaluate the distance and the ball's weight, which requires some skill. Playing this game can be beneficial for many reasons. Physical activity, fresh air and the sociable aspects are only a few. You stretch your muscles, train your balance and sense of distance and most of all relax quietly. Get an anti-stress boule set now.

Collect your favourite gang, head to the nearest park or square and instead of having another coffee or beer, enjoy a game of boule.

CHESS

Benjamin Franklin, one of the Founding Fathers of the United States, wrote that "The game of chess is not merely an idle amusement; several very valuable qualities of the mind, useful in the course of human life, are to be acquired and strengthened by it, so as to become habits ready on all occasions". We may learn not only as Franklin stressed: foresight, circumspection or caution, but also how to breathe a bit of slowness into our lives. Chess is far from boring or doing nothing. It is all about a strategy and tactics.

The game was most probably born in Eastern India, where it was known in the 6th century under the name chaturanga. The Silk Road trade routes helped it travel further. Chess was played in Persia, where it was introduced by the Arabic culture after the conquest. After reaching Europe and spreading in around the 9th century, the game's rules were modified and finally standardized in the 19th century.

What is the philosophy of chess? You need two players and a square board with eight rows (called ranks) and eight columns (files). This grid is a playground for two sets of pieces (one white, one black). Each set consists of 1 king, 1 queen, 2 rooks, 2 knights, 2 bishops and 8 pawns. As each piece in the chess set moves in a particular way, the biggest challenge is to learn rules of the movements. Through practice you develop a strategy and the ability to foresee your opponent's moves. Even if you are experienced, some games go on for up to several hours. If you don't have company, you can try to play with your computer. Specially developed programmes can be challenging. One managed in 1997 to defeat Garry Kasparov, who is regarded as the greatest chess player of all time. Checkmate!

Learn the rules and
master them patiently.
Buy a portable set to
celebrate the art of
chess while travelling.

TENT

Having a tent with you is like moving around on a bike. You are entirely independent, can go anywhere (and on budget!) and if you wish you can stop at any time. Few routes and not many places are inaccessible for you and above all, you are close to the nature. Spending a night in a tent is an alluring idea, it sounds like an adventure. How much fun it is you will only know if you try it.

The placement of the tent's structure requires some skill, but is not that difficult. It must be correctly supported by the poles and fastened by pegs stuck firmly into the ground. Nowadays, you can select among many types and styles of lightweight and trekking tents. Dome, tunnel, pyramid or geodesic designs are all equipped with flexible poles and made of innovative materials. Unlike the traditional Inuit tent, called 'tupiq' and created from seal or caribou skins, advanced technology offers breathable solutions. Travellers can plan their excursions more easily. The tents are much lighter, quicker to set up and resistant to variable weather conditions. In the wilderness it is crucial to have equipment you can depend on as the weather may change rapidly. Together with a sleeping bag, the tent provides you with shelter for the night and makes you feel comfortable.

We travel extensively, but often don't pay attention to the details. Setting off on a backpacking journey with a tent requires awareness. The slow course it dictates allows time to appreciate the surroundings, fresh air and freedom. You feel connected with the place where you camp as well as with the people with whom you share the tent. There are no distractions, just you and nature. This adventurous experience, especially in our ultra-modern world, will be recreational as well as refreshing.

Plan a weekend in nature with a sleep-over in a tent. If you cannot go anywhere far, ask if you can set up a tent in a friend's or family garden.

OPTIMA

PICNIC BASKET

The ability to eat in the open air is one of the most pleasant aspects of summer. The concept of a picnic is also probably the most picturesque option. In the past the picnic was reserved exclusively for the aristocracy, it inspired works of many writers and artists. Romantic novels, Jane Austen's among others, were filled with numerous meals eaten outdoors. Manet's 'The Luncheon on the Grass' may have caused controversy because of the female nude, but for decades has been a typical example of an idyllic rural scene. Even film directors employ the trope, such as Peter Weir in his famous movie from 1975 telling the story of a group of schoolgirls and their teacher who mysteriouslt disappear in Picnic at Hanging Rock.

A picnic successfully fuses the pleasure of appreciating food and nature. Invented for lazy sessions *en plein air* including unhurried conversation, light meals and wine tasting, reading and even taking a nap. Charming scenery is essential, as well as the proper setting, a large blanket and often cushions for more comfort do the trick. However you cannot have a picnic without a proper picnic basket. Plates, cutlery, glasses, napkins, a cloth or wine opener will be very useful in making the best of an excursion on a warm and sunny day.

Organized within a family or circle of friends, a picnic can also have more sportive elements. Running after a drifting kite, kicking a ball, playing badminton or enjoying other outdoor games will help burn calories. Some people decide to bring food with them and others to cook the food outside on a barbecue. There is no way to consider about speed during a picnic. So it is better to equip yourself with a picnic basket and use it whenever the weather allows.

Plan a picnic: check the weather forecast and adjust the menu to the participants' tastes. Select a scenic place with a picturesque view and pack your picnic basket.

ICE BAG®

After a long and tiring day at work, and for many, an even more exhausting commute, there comes a moment to enjoy some relaxation. Especially during long summer evenings, a glass of rosé or white wine can do magic. Enjoying the wine's taste is a formidable method for implementing slowness into your life. There is only one major condition – the wine should be properly cooled. We are used to the sight of buckets filled with ice cubes next to a restaurant table, but can we afford the same luxury at home?

Ice bag® was developed in 2003 and is a durable yet very light PVC bag made of recyclable material. It is easy to carry at home, on picnics or holidays. When empty, it can be folded and stored using minimal space. It seems much more practical than a bucket. Originally created for champagne bottles, it is still used to deliver cold bubbles, but being so universal it suits wine as well. The revelation is that it chills faster than a traditional ice bucket and keeps its temperature longer on a hot day. You can even buy a bottle on your way to a dinner at someone's house and bring it in an Ice bag® for immediate consumption. It comes in a version with partitions that can hold up to 4 bottles (that would be the model you need for bigger parties).

The concept is simple, but how inventive! The product was developed through a process of many experiments (and protected by trademark law) and is available in many models and colors. It is a trendy and useful accessory to have at home.

Invent something tasty and light for dinner. While preparing it, put a bottle of wine into an Ice bag®. Slooooow down in the company of deliciously cooled wine.

TABLE

Be it a home, office or a restaurant, a table is the centre of their spaces. Whether it is located in a kitchen, a dining or living room (some flats merge these into one space), this is where we sit when we want to spend time with others. A conversation during a meal sharing a table is one of the most valuable parts of family and social life. At work, even if everyone has their own desk, anything that requires brainstorming or common arrangements takes place at a big table. Like a pitch for football players, this is where the team belongs. In restaurants there are more and more communal tables that allow strangers to eat side by side. It is a pleasant option, especially if you are eating by yourself. A large table will not allow you feel lonely as there is lots of space for others to join.

A table is synonymous with community. We spend a lot of time at it with colleagues, friends or family working, discussing, eating and celebrating things together. It attracts like a magnet and becomes the best platform for meeting and exchanging ideas. An equivalent of Twitter, in reality, we share news, information and ideas. Regardless of the shape of the table, it magically gathers a group of people and focuses their attention on each other.

Eating on the run, often while standing and alone, are sadly signs of our times. We suggest an attractive alternative. Focus on the table, regard it as an incredibly important piece of furniture, a central piece of furnishing. Let it dictate to you the slow style of life. Introduce new habits, like celebrating meals and inviting others to share them with you. Take your time to enjoy both food and company.

Organize a big dinner. If you do not own a large table, merge smaller ones. Focus not only on the food you are going to serve, but also the way you will decorate the table (and don't expect your guests to leave before midnight).

BARBECUE
BBQ

Grilling or smoking meat, fish, or vegetables dates back to the cave age – and has been popular ever since – think about the taste of a grilled sausage and you will feel how irresistible BBQ is. While modern barbecue culture and utensils emerged in the United States in the 19th century, the idea of grilling fresh or marinated ingredients on sticks or on a grate and enjoying the special taste resulting from the slow cooking on charcoal, is probably universal. It is a fundamental part of traditional Korean cuisine, and similarly, you cannot imagine Cajun food without BBQ.

A barbecue party is associated with festive events (such as July 4th in the US), with informal socializing and summer. A good mood, a relaxed atmosphere and abundant food are key ingredients to its success. While you can find countless high-tech barbecues using gas, fuel or even electricity as a source of heat, the best barbecue is still the original one using charcoal – you actually do not need the apparatus, just a couple of stones assembled properly around a campfire are enough – but do make sure to secure the place to avoid damaging the surroundings. Curiously, barbecuing is an activity popular with men – unlike cooking indoors. Barbecuing does not require any particular skills, just a lot of patience and attention, and allows you to have a drink with friends while the food is cooking.

Barbecue is not fast food; it is part of the ritual to have the taste buds excited by the smell of food grilling slowly. Remember that the most important is to enjoy the party, meet with neighbours or people you would never chat with otherwise, feel the freedom of eating outdoors and having good time.

If you have a garden do it at your place, if not, find a park with specially designated areas and enjoy the taste of grilled meat, fish or vegetables.

COOKBOOK

Cooking together with friends can be quite fun. It can show a lot about the personality of each participant; you easily see who sticks to the rules or who likes improvising and innovating, for example. The immense diversity of cookbooks allows for countless culinary experiments, from hearty, traditional dishes you loved in your childhood to exotic meals that will surprise and charm your senses with their subtle aromas. If you are lucky enough to have inherited your parents' or grandparents' cookbooks, you may plunge into a nostalgic trip, and perhaps find their handwritten annotations and variants.

Unlike in the past, modern cookbooks are richly illustrated and lavishly designed. They combine detailed recipes and photographs or drawings showing the different phases of preparation. They make great presents for gourmets and people curious about food. Cookbooks dedicated to culinary traditions of a particular region or country are fantastic guides for armchair travelers. It is great to explore a place through its specialties and art de vivre, and these cookbooks usually offer an original insight into the lifestyle of a country .The illustrations give you a foretaste of what you will eat and some inspiration when you feel tired of everyday food. It is always exciting to try something new and challenging, and cooking is an artistic activity – you take raw material and transform it into a work with aesthetic, gustative, and nutritive value.

Three or four generations in a family can take part in cooking, as it is an enjoyable pastime for children and seniors alike. Cooking and then eating together is a great way to celebrate both your relations and good food. It does not have to be a sophisticated recipe; although the more original, the more interesting. Even easy and simple ideas inspired by cookbooks can be fun.

Go through your cookbooks at home and find something tasty that you have never cooked before.

Invite friends, family or loved ones and try out the recipe or prepare the food together. Bon appétit!

PHOTO ALBUM

We take an overwhelming number of photos these days. Back in the 19th century when photography was invented, it was a revelation. People finally had a way to save the memory of their loved ones, events or places. Today there is a camera in nearly every electronic device. We take pictures with our smartphones anytime we spot something that we find interesting to save (for some of us it equals almost everything). Digital technology has made it possible to store hundreds or even thousands of them on hard discs or in 'the cloud'. Due to the unbelievable number of photos we take, we rarely print them anymore. Looked at on the screens of computers and phones, with time they are forgotten or deleted as quickly as they were taken.

Surely we miss the spirit of photography as it was invented, so why don't we try to do it the old way? In the non-digital world where cameras used film with a limited number of shots, much more time was required to consider what was really worthwhile capturing. In addition, the fact that the film had to be developed and the photos printed made the process longer and more thoughtful. Recorded moments really meant something as they were carefully selected.

It was usual to print copies of the best photos and to arrange them in a photo album, later leafing slowly through the pages which could take us on a sentimental journey into the past. Some of our memorable moments could be relived, people who played an important role in our life cherished and places we visited recalled. Even if we keep on using digital cameras, we can at least implement the analog scheme by being more selective in what we capture and printing the images to create photo albums so that we can enjoy the visual archive mindfully and bring back the charm of photography.

On the occasion of the next family reunion, ask everyone to bring some photo albums. Gathered in one place they will tell a handful of stories about the past. Cherish them slowly.

TO ENTE

AIN

BOOK

Francis George Steiner used to say that books are "the best antidote against the marsh-gas of boredom and vacuity." They are great friends and if selected well they will always keep you company and entertain you. Some books can be dangerous, as they may change your life, let you see things differently or discover something new about yourself. Also, "Books force you to give something back to them, to exercise your intelligence and imagination" (Paul Auster). Discovering new facts or ways of seeing the world and exploring the complexity of people's emotions through various stories can offer valuable lessons. While books can transport you magically from the real world into a world of stories and characters, they also teach us how to live and evolve.

As American novelist George Raymond Richard Martin said: "A reader lives a thousand lives before he dies, the man who never reads lives only one". Books are like chocolate, you do not even notice when you are highly addicted. The fear of running out of things to read is called abibliophobia. Avid readers who do not go anywhere without at least one volume in their bag or pocket can be described with the phrase book-bosomed, coined by Walter Scott.

Reading a book is like celebrating the moment, switching into the slow mode as you turn the pages. It means forgetting about other issues, worries or plans and immersing yourself into another reality, enjoying the expressions and reflections without hurrying. Any bookshelf is like Harry Potter's platform 9¾ at King's Cross Station, as soon as you take a book and start reading it, you will be transported to another world, different each time.

Organise your time so that you have 30 minutes for reading daily. Make a small ritual of it: a cup of hot chocolate or refreshing ice tea depending on the time of the year (and either a blanket or a fan accordingly), comfortable seat and if it is after dark, a good lamp!

MAPS

The world's oldest map comes from a cave in Abauntz in the Spanish Navarra region and was carved on a stone tablet 14,000 years ago. People have always had a strong need to map the planet. First their closest neighbourhood and with time every continent. Looking at historical maps sketched over the centuries, one witnesses the fascinating process of discovering the world by famous explorers.

Cartography is the art or technique of making maps requiring a fusion of science, technique and aesthetics. The foundations of the discipline were set out for the first time in around 150 AD by Claudius Ptolemy, a Greek scholar living in Alexandria, whose 'Geography' was based on math as well as geography. He invented a system of rectangles and intersecting lines to map the globe and describe the latitude and longitude for many locations. Cartography has always kept up with technological innovations to make maps more and more precise. The digital revolution took the art of mapping to a new level. Nothing can compare with either the accuracy we have achieved, or the wide availability of maps.

Navigation and finding one's whereabouts was never as easy as it is today. GPS (Global Positioning System), especially the systems we have in our cars and mobile phones, often rescues us from getting lost and suggests the quickest route from point A to point B. On the other hand the more technology we use, the less cartographic consciousness we have. Even if in today's digitalized world, a traditional map does not sound very sexy, they do have a lot of charm and offer mindful travelling. Finding your whereabouts requires thinking, terrain orientation and awareness during the trip, but at least you participate in it fully and thus make the best of it.

LYON
Tarare
Pontcharra
L'Arbresle
Sain-Bel
Bessenay
Violay
Montrottier
Panissières
St-Laurent-de-Ch.
Vaugneray
Yzeron
Thurins
Brignais
St-Martin-en-H.
Mornant
Givors
Duerne
Ste-Foy-l'A.
St-Symphorien
Heyrieux
Chaponnay
Vienne
Pont-Evêque
N89
D89
N86
A7
D75

Leave your mobile GPS at home and set off on a journey armed only with a traditional map. It will be a take-your-time kind of adventure. Explore without rushing.

B 1 2 5 10 25 50 100 200 400
3,5 ft
m
20 50 INF ∞
5 7 9 12 20 20
1,5 2 3 4 7

ANALOGUE CAMERA

The moment when photography switched from analogue to digital was a game changer. The new technology brought the possibility of encoding and storing images digitally. The Internet's wide possibilities enhanced further changes. And so billion of photos are taken every day, with cameras, smartphones or iPads, which end up in the vast online space. These significant changes introduced totally new behaviours. We tend to interact with the surrounding reality and with each other through images. With Internet connectivity practically ubiquitous, we also upload a massive number of photos. Social media (and their users) love the flow of imagery. A total of 300 million photos per day are uploaded to Facebook (which means approx. 136,000 photos every 60 seconds!).

Now let's take a look back. Photography was born on both sides of the La Manche Channel at nearly the same time. In France around 1826/27, Joseph Nicéphore Niépce took a photo called 'View from a window at Le Gras', which is regarded as the earliest known photograph. Just a couple of years later, the Englishman William Henry Fox Talbot, who was experimenting with various techniques, created a photo of the library window at his home Lacock Abbey. It is said to be the oldest negative in existence.

Through a series of fascinating experiments they started the beautiful art of creating images by recording light. Traditional techniques require time, you have to learn how to adjust the exposure time and set the lens. It also takes longer to see the result, which does not appear on the screen at once. First a roll of film has to be developed. Instead of 50 photos you take one, so you pay more attention to looking at what you are photographing. Instead of endless repetitions and thoughtless shutter releasing, you take your time. An analogue camera is thus the perfect tool to ease you into a slow mode.

Give your digital camera(s) a day off and try to take some photos with an analogue model.

GRAMOPHONE

The charm of the characteristic, slightly creaky sound of a gramophone's stylus reading the disc's circular groove, turns listening to music into a unique experience. The gramophone was invented in 1877by Thomas Edison, one of the most prolific inventors in history. Previous experiments led to devices that were able to record some sounds, but Edison's invention was actually the first one to reproduce the recorded sound. His phonograph underwent many developments. In the 1880s Alexander Graham Bell introduced a cut stylus that followed a zig zag groove in the record. The next decade brought the flat discs with a spiral groove that we know today (invented by Emile Berliner). The stylus, disc size, speeds as well as drive and equalization systems were also modified over the years to come. From around the 1950s it became common to have a record player at home.

The fact that you could record music and re-play the sounds brought a revolution and started the music business. Although they seem vintage, vinyl records have actually been used since the gramophone inception and are still in use today. Of course the new formats like cassette tape and then compact disc as well as digital recording made vinyl records less common for a while, but their popularity is growing again and all recently released records are available in this format (loved by DJs). In case you collect vinyl records, remember that while they are not prone to breaking, it is easy to scratch their surface, which also gathers dust and should not be exposed to sunlight.

A gramophone adds authenticity and a special character no matter what kind of music one listens to. Music from a gramophone stops being just the background noise, in a way it is so present that it requires your full and unhurried attention.

Organize a gramophone evening. Sit comfortably with your guests around a gramophone, select vinyls that will please everyone.

POTTER'S WHEEL

You want to free your mind? Try working with your hands, it is one of the best ways to soothe tensions. It will not only be handwork, but also create an object that you can actually use. Get messy with clay and eliminate stress through an artistic activity that requires a lot of time and attention. It is a machine associated with artists or art students, but you don't have to be one in order to develop ceramic objects and benefit from the potter's wheel salutary impact.

In the Egyptian mythology, one of the most ancient gods is Khnum. Ruling over all water, he was also responsible for delivering black silt to the Nile's banks to improve fertility. The silt was also the material used to make pottery and so Khnum was believed to have moulded all of creation including human beings and the other gods with a potter's wheel. Historians have several hypotheses about the invention of the potter's wheel. Some suggest it was developed in Mesopotamia, others point to the Indus Valley in South Asia or to evidence mentioning Egypt. In every case we are speaking about times as far back as 3500-3000 BC.

The basic principle is that you form a body from a lump of clay placed centrally on the top of a rotating mould. You work with the material, squeeze it and lift it to give it a shape. The mass of the heavy stone wheel is either kicked or pushed around to keep moving. There are two types of technique – 'jiggering' for flat ware, like plates and 'jollying' for hollow objects, like cups or vases. At the beginning not all attempts are successful. The clay has tendency to splash around, particularly when how you work with your hands is not attuned with the wheel's rhythm. Do not rush then.

Find a workshop you could join to learn this relaxing activity. Find out which objects you enjoy making most.

POTS FOR HERBS

When you master the technique of pot making you can begin to think of this next step – herbs garden at home. Some of us are lucky enough to have a garden next to the house, but those who are less lucky have to find other solutions to grow fresh plants. By creating a small plantation at home, you can have tasty and healthy additions to your meals independent of the weather, all year round! Imagine: dill, fennel, oregano, rosemary, sage, tarragon, thyme, parsley, garlic, mint, coriander or basil within your reach. While gardening is reasonably easy and relaxing, there are several things to consider and rules to follow.

First of all, you have to decide where to place the pots. There are a couple of options, like a balcony (or a winter garden if you have one) or simply a windowsill in the kitchen. Depending on the location, select the best containers to grow your herbs in – the shapes should be adjusted to the space you have available (don't forget about the aesthetic aspect!). They should have some holes in the bottom to drain well. Another important thing is to use a high quality and loose soil, which will need fertilizing from time to time. As for watering, you have to watch the plants and how they behave. If the soil becomes dry and pale, add a reasonable amount of water once or twice a day or as needed. If it feels moist and has a fresh colour, skip the watering.

Planning a garden and taking care of it will certainly teach you how to slow down at home. Plus contact with nature, even on such a small scale can be beneficial. Get inspired by ideas on how to style your collection of herb pots from social media and then get to work!

Start your own home garden, either for the kitchen or your balcony. Adjust pots size accordingly and plant herbs that you use most while cooking.

OFF
ON

SEWING MACHINE

Aren't you fed up with shopping in the same chain stores available everywhere? Or hunting for sales? And seeing the same clothes you wear on every second person in the street? Wouldn't you prefer to have an individual look and fill your wardrobe with unique pieces? If you answered 'yes' to these questions, it is high time to think about a sewing machine. Imagine if all the rush and anxiety that accompany looking for and trying on clothes disappeared. You could use all your imagination to create something original without the stress.

The origins of the sewing machine include several people and many experiments. However the first functional sewing machine was invented and patented in 1830 by a French tailor, Barthelemy Thimonnier. Four years later Walter Hunt in America constructed a machine using two spools of thread and incorporated an eye-pointed needle for stitching, but the first patent for a device using thread from two different sources was issued in America in 1846 to Elias Howe. Sewing machines finally went into mass production in the 1850s, when Isaac Singer completed a model with a needle moving up and down powered by a foot treadle. It was a huge commercial success and a 'Singer' is the most iconic sewing machine ever.

It takes time to sew anything, but the pleasure of having something original, self-designed and tailor-made is rewarding. When using a sewing machine you have to be very patient and careful, otherwise you can easily destroy the needles or the fabrics. It requires concentration and focus, thanks to which you will calm down. Instead of stressful visits to shops, you can enjoy a romance with fashion on a different level. Who knows? Perhaps sewing will be so enjoyable that you will decide to launch your own label. Today everything is possible!

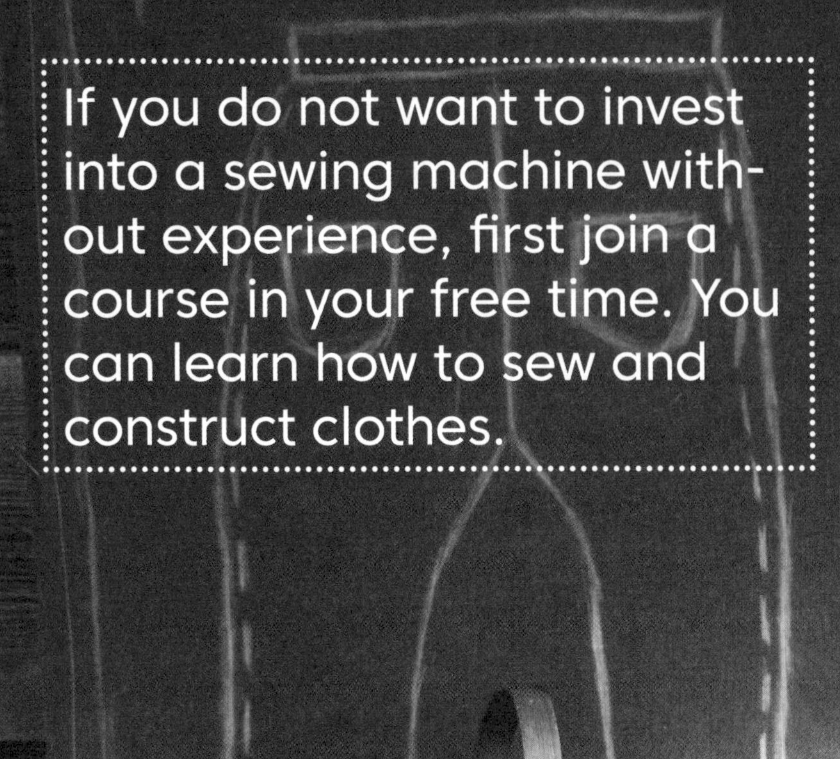

If you do not want to invest into a sewing machine without experience, first join a course in your free time. You can learn how to sew and construct clothes.

COLOURING BOOK

Colouring books, one of best parts of the childhood, are now officially allowed for grown-ups. The craze is massive. Bookshops share as many shelves and tables for displaying them as for other books. Their popularity was so big that at one stage the manufacturers producing the colouring pencils were not able to fulfil the huge number of orders on time. Publishers are in fierce competition in the race for new ideas to surprise the clients with something fresh and interesting. In terms of themes, adults can find any subject they could dream of, be it floral motifs, animal patterns, geometric compositions, famous cities, fashion sketches, stories inspired by famous novels or writers. The newest trend is group colouring. Identical to book clubs, people meet either in homes or cafés and fill in printed patterns while talking and enjoying each other's company.

Colouring in adulthood has many positive properties. As the patterns are much more complex and detailed than the ones for children, they require a lot of patience. Secondly, because the designs to colour are either harmonious or simply charming, the activity is highly calming and entertaining. Focusing on the simple, yet stimulating activity of selecting colours and filling in the shapes can be a source of inner balance and peace. Another great thing about colouring books is that they are a way to improve creativity as well as increase concentration. The more you exercise both, the stronger they will get.

Regardless of the subject, a colouring book is an anti-stress experience. You take time to colour complex pictures (some templates are truly sophisticated), so it is almost like meditating. You please your senses and enjoy relaxation.

Forget about issues of daily life, grab colouring pencils, select the patterns you find most inspiring, play some relaxing music and let your imagination run free.

XXL JIGSAW PUZZLE

Solving a XXL jigsaw puzzle may bring back some long-forgotten memories of your childhood, when putting together a jigsaw puzzle was one of your favorite activities. Their educational value is impressive. Not only will you learn to spot various shapes and colours, but also to assemble them patiently, using your imagination and observation skills to assemble the pieces.

If you are stressed or are lacking the ability to concentrate, a XXL jigsaw puzzle (with at least 500 pieces) is a perfect tool to make you focus on its elements, offering you a relaxing distraction from your other worries. You may not manage to solve the puzzle at once, but you can end a session whenever you wish, and resume it with renewed energy and a refreshed brain. You can select the image you want to re-create from among thousands of pictures: from posters of iconic movies to animals, landscapes, seascapes, portraits and so many more. Assembling the elements makes you feel like an old master of Dutch painting, adding small details to small details to form a colourful, and lively composition.

Jigsaw puzzles became popular in the 18th century and derive from geographical maps. They were originally made of wooden pieces, but cardboard puzzles are more common these days. Some XXL jigsaw puzzles
offer pictures with optical illusions, which make them even more of a challenge to assemble It is an ideal game whether you are on your own, with families, or groups of friends. They are recommended to seniors as a memorizing exercise. It is a perfect pastime for a rainy day, or a long evening in the winter, such as after a day skiing. The body can relax while the brain is playing, and there is a particular pride in putting in the final piece.

Get the biggest XXL jigsaw puzzle with an image you like. Be it a cityscape or a landscape or an animal, you can solve it on your own or invite some friends. Remember to take time to match all the pieces.

BALLOON

This is probably the biggest and most extraordinary tool for slow living in our selection. Human beings have always dreamt of being able to fly. No wonder, the idea of feeling free high in the sky is very tempting. Leonardo da Vinci, inspired by nature, had already worked on machines that could let a man possess the power of a bird. Improvements on his invention over many centuries resulted in airplanes that gave us a foretaste of flight on spread wings, yet we are trapped inside a structure. Sure, there is also parachuting which provides real contact with nature and beautiful views, as well as a rush of adrenaline. But nothing is more exciting and, in a way, romantic than the slow flight of a hot-air balloon.

The first European balloon flight is believed to have happened in 1709 in Lisbon, when the Brazilian-Portuguese priest and scientist Bartolomeu Lourenço de Gusmão succeeded in lifting a small paper balloon four meters (13 feet) above the ground in front of King John V and the Portuguese court. Yet the real fame of launching ballooning belongs to French inventors the Montgolfier brothers. In September 1783, an experiment with animals (a sheep, a duck and a rooster to be precise) sent up in a balloon to the altitude of 460 meters (1,500 feet) and a distance of 3 kilometers (two miles) for around eight minutes (watched by King Louis XVI and Queen Marie-Antoinette) landed safely. The brothers performed the very first free flight involving humans in November the same year. Two passengers flew for 25 minutes.

Today hot air balloons have much more advanced heat sources and are used mainly for recreation. There are certain regions where ballooning is particularly popular due to spectacular landscapes, such as Cappadocia in Turkey, where you can admire orchards, vineyards and picturesque valleys from above.

If you are not afraid of heights and the idea of sitting in a basket suspended hundreds of meters above the ground does not freak you out, check out where you can enjoy this special experience in your area. If going up in a balloon is too much for your nerves, you can always watch this beautiful spectacle from the ground.

CREDITS

All photos Shutterstock: cover © DotExe; pp. 2 © MartiniDry; 9 © Anna Tamila; 10-11 © Oleksandr Liesnoi; 12 © Rawpixel.com; 14-15 © Pete Pahham; 17 © Peter Wooton; 18-19 © Nick Hawkes; 20 © Franz Peter Rudolf; 22-23 © Dudarev Mikhail; 24 © Blazej Lyjak; 26-27 © blurAZ; 29 © Floral Deco; 30-31 © Soloviova Liudmyla; 33 © Leifstiller; 34-35 © Hans Magelssen; 36 © Jodie Johnson; 38-39 © wavebreak-media; 40 © Suradech Prapairat; 42-43 © pixfly; 45 © takoburito; 46-47 © Poprotskiy Alexey; 49 © WorldWide; 50-51, 52, 146-147 © Photographee.eu; 54-55 © All About Space; 57 © LightField Studios; 58-59 © holbox; 60-61 © Merydolla; 62 © Photology1971; 64-65 © 2M media; 67 © Yulia Grigoryeva; 68-69 © Pavel Vakhrushev; 71 © Lindsay Helms; 72-73 © Ditty_about_sum-mer; 74 © Katya Havok; 76-77 © GaudiLab; 78, 80-81 © B Brown; 82 © Guschenkova; 84-85 © leungc-hopan; 87 © Indypendenz; 88-89 © jakkapan; 90 © Jacob Lund; 92-93 © Christian Delbert; 94 © Daboost; 99 © Skumer; 100-101 © Ambient Ideas; 102, 186 © Andrekart Photog-raphy; 104-105 © mama_mia; 107 © Oleksandr Kavun; 108-109 © Gita Kulinitch Studio; 111 © sirtravelalot; 112-113 © Maridav; 115 © Refat; 116-117 © LemmeArt; 118-119, 145 © Rasta777; 120 © dimbar76; 122-123 © Philip Lange; 124 © Mrak hr; 126-127 © Bjoern Wylezich; 129 © White78; 130-131 © librakv; 132 © Dmitry Naumov; 134-135 © Feel good studio; 136 © Versta; 138-139 © Stock-Asso; 140 © AT; 142-143, 188-189 © Shaiith; 148 © Sebastian Duda; 150-151 © FreeProd33; 153 © VICUSCHKA; 154-155 © Evgeny Karandaev; 157 © KC Slagle; 158-159 © Stocknapper; 160-161 © Dmi-triy Strekachev; 163 © MaskaRad; 164-165 © Mladen Mitrinovic; 167 © Gemenacom; 168-169 © Yuganov Konstantin; 170 © Tompet; 172-173 © Pathara Buranadilok; 175 © Lari-na Marina; 176-177 © tomertu; 178 © Kalamurzing; 180-181 © wave-breakmedia; 183 © Image17; 184-185 © natalia bulatova; 191-193 © ABO PHOTOGRAPHY; 195 © Yulia_ Bogomolova; 196-197 © ampcool; 198 © Igor Zh.; 200-201 © Olena Tur; 203 © Alena Ozerova; 204-205 © nioloxs; 206 © Africa Studio; 208 © WorkingPens.

Created by:

FANCY
BOOKS

www.fancy-books-packaging.com

Copyediting: Lee Ripley
Layout & Cover Design: Fancy Books Packaging

Printed in Estonia, 2017

ISBN 978-1-908233-01-1

Eken Press Ltd. is a company registered in England and Wales under the number 7454591.
Follow us on ekenpress.com.

FIND
joy
IN
THE
ORDINARY